Augustus Craven

A noble lady

(Adelaide Capece Minutolo)

Augustus Craven

A noble lady
(Adelaide Capece Minutolo)

ISBN/EAN: 9783741181719

Manufactured in Europe, USA, Canada, Australia, Japa

Cover: Foto ©Andreas Hilbeck / pixelio.de

Manufactured and distributed by brebook publishing software (www.brebook.com)

Augustus Craven

A noble lady

A NOBLE LADY.

If the fresh waters, which from living Fount
Distil their sweetness into noble Souls,
Should burst in rills and fertilise the world ;
Earth's best and wisest then, in love with Love,
Would grasp their Cross and climb the mountain-peak,
To taste Life's sweetness when it mates with Death ;
Nor only when eternal joy foreshines,
But when to leave life's shadows stings the soul.

Vittoria Colonna.

A NOBLE LADY

(ADELAIDE CAPECE MINUTOLO).

BY

MRS. AUGUSTUS CRAVEN.

Translated, at the Author's request,

By EMILY BOWLES.

LONDON:
BURNS, OATES, AND COMPANY,
17 & 18 Portman Street, and 63 Paternoster Row.
1869.

TO

MY FOUR SISTERS;

WHOSE LOVING UNION HAS

BROUGHT FORTH STRENGTH AND SWEETNESS;

𝔗his little 𝔅ook is offered.

A NOBLE LADY

(ADELAIDE CAPECE MINUTOLO).

CHAPTER I.

"DEATH is the real mirror of life," says a grand Christian of the seventeenth century;* and these words are still true, even when the shadow of death hinders the survivors from discerning their whole ground of hope. But when this shadow is scattered, and nothing clouds the dread and truthful mirror of the last hour—when God permits us to behold the soul of a friend reflected therein, himself, and yet more than himself—the same as when we loved him in life, yet already transfigured by the forerunning brightness of a better world

* The Marquis de Mérode-Treion.

—when exceptional and terrible sufferings only serve to bring out what he has been throughout the length of a happy life—then, instead of suffering the anguish of a mournful farewell, the heart bounds with the hope of eternal reward, and joyfully acknowledges yet once again that the love of God is not only Heaven itself, but that in this world too His love softens the bitterest grief, and transfigures even death in its hour.

It was in this way that Adelaide Capece Minutolo, of the illustrious house of the princes of Canosa, ended her life at Naples the beginning of this present year.* A noble life, whose Christian simplicity bore the germ of her heroic death, and bequeathed to those who stood by her deathbed feelings of consolation which no words can convey. The following pages, therefore, are not addressed to them, for they need them not. But what served to comfort them

* 1869.

will also instruct us; what added to their fortitude will strengthen our weakness; and as after battle it is thought well to inspire courage by speaking of those who fought valiantly, so in the battle of life, which we all must wage, it is a good and wholesome thing to watch how brave souls bear themselves; the more specially if they do not belong to those chosen ranks who lead the van, and whose deeds we would fain persuade ourselves are only examples for the few, but are among those who have fought and conquered with ourselves, have mingled with the crowd, and marched in the field at our side.

CHAPTER II.

ADELAIDE'S lot in life was not an extraordinary one, and yet it was remarkable on one account, which was, that she chose out her own path of happiness, and walked in it according to that choice; whereas it tended in neither of the two directions which in general, and especially in Italy, are the only roads open to women—she did not become a nun, and she never married.

At the opening of her young life, her father's death having brought about some reverse of fortune, she had been early trained to thoughtfulness and self-restraint, to bear with cheerful courage the deprivation of the pleasures of her age, and to preserve an equal mind amid those changes which merely affect the outward aspect of life. I shall not dwell, moreover, upon a period when Adelaide was in nowise distinguished from her sisters Pauline and Clotilde. During the early years of their lives she was exactly what they were—brave, happy in the perfect union that reigned between themselves, and in the passionate love they showed for their mother,* whose devotedness, capacity, and indomitable energy, seconded by the eagerness with which the sacrifices she required were accepted by her children, succeeded finally in recovering their fortunes. After many years of retirement, her daughters were just about to reappear in the world and assume the position suitable to their birth, when the one great sorrow of her life struck Adelaide to the ground. After a last voyage to Andalusia to settle her children's affairs, the Marchioness di Minutolo

* Mathilde de Galvez, Marchioness of Capece Minutolo, daughter of Bernard, first Count de Galvez, Viceroy of Mexico in 1785, niece and heiress to the Marquis de la Sonora, Indian Minister under Charles III. (*Note.*)

was attacked by a rapid and dangerous illness, to which she fell a victim in a few days; and her daughters, who had gone with her, returned to Naples orphans.

This frightful blow, coming at the same moment with the final arrangement of their affairs, left them entirely, though sorrowfully, free; and it was then that Adelaide took that line which was so significative of her whole character.

Pauline, the eldest sister, had just accepted an offer of marriage from Francis del Balzo, the Marquis de la Sonora.

And in like manner Adelaide, if she had wished it, could easily have married suitably to her station; but at this juncture she calmly looked life in the face, and examined herself as to the conditions under which she could secure happiness. She perceived, therefore, distinctly, that, as far as she was concerned, happiness must comprise peace; the sympathetic union of two hearts and minds, with such a conformity of tastes and equality of wills as should enable her to walk in a course which, without being exceptional, should constantly tend upwards and towards God. She discerned also that, instead of seeking such an ideal in the doubtful realisation of marriage, and the keener joys and splendours of the world, she possessed its elements at home, and required nothing more.

Clotilde, her youngest sister, was bound to her by that similarity of tastes which fulfilled all her conditions of happiness: the sisters therefore mutually resolved to seek nothing further than to live together, determining, with one accord, not to marry, and never to separate from each other while they lived. Opportunities of changing her mind were offered to Adelaide some time afterwards under circumstances which might both have touched her heart and dazzled her pride; but nothing ever induced her to waver, nor did either of them ever feel a regret, or doubt the wisdom of their choice, till, at the end of eight-and-twenty years, death dissolved their union.

CHAPTER III.

BEFORE the sisters could settle their life according to their plan, it was necessary to undergo some struggles; for neither in Italy nor in France is there any place reserved in the world—in the "great world," above all —for unmarried women. When it so happens that the daughter of a family receives no suitable offer, and death deprives her of her natural protectors, it is necessary for her to find some other; and in return for that countenance which she is not allowed to be without, she is obliged sometimes to accept conditions hard enough to justify in some measure the general aversion to old maids. To them time neither brings freedom nor even loosens the shackles forged to protect their youth, but which equally fetter them in advanced life.

This was the antique custom of society from which Adelaide strove to escape by "founding the Institution of Old Maids at Naples." She did this in fact, and succeeded in obtaining the independence she sought for herself and her sister. They first settled in Naples, and afterwards at Posilippo, in a villa whose enchanting position engraves it upon the memory of all who are acquainted with the Bay of Naples. In 1818 this villa, which stands upon one of the promontories of the Strada Nuova, was given by Ferdinand I. to the Margravine of Anspach, then living at Naples, and who had built upon this tongue of land a kind of pavilion resembling a small Greek temple, which stood in a garden running down to the sea, and which, backed by trees and surrounded by flowers, formed a pretty object either from the sea or land, and still figures in every view of the Bay of Naples drawn from 1818 to 1851. In the latter year, Mr. Keppel Craven, the son and heir of the

Margravine, bequeathed the pavilion and garden to the two sisters Minutolo, to whom he had been a most faithful and constant friend. When they had remodelled the little temple, it lost its primitive character; but they made it into a convenient and graceful dwelling, which now became their only place of abode; where for many years they spent a peaceful and occupied life, and where they fulfilled their dream of happiness, which was to be bought, like every best earthly gift, by the voluntary and full sacrifice of some earthly joys.

There is no doubt that this kind of happiness did not appear enviable to every one; and among the numerous friends who for many years visited them in retirement, there would doubtless be some joyous and much-loved wife, some proud and fond mother, and especially more than one frivolous companion, who would declare that they could not endure to spend their days and grow old in such a way of life.

But this impression was still somewhat a rare one. It is not often that perfect happiness is found in this world, and when we find it, both the heart and eye recognise it and enjoy its repose. How many times have we ourselves not so rested in that spot, where religion, friendship, art, and literary pursuits all seemed to have met together, framed, as it were, by the most glorious natural scenery, and where the soul and heart, the understanding and the eye, were alike satisfied! Without wounding the vanity of one who lived for and in her, we may say that Adelaide was the centre of that circle; that not only were her talents remarkable, but her mind, like her character, had somewhat of that manly strain which had perhaps come down to her through her mother's Spanish blood. In this way, together with wonderful sweetness, great simplicity, and matchless tenderness of character, she not only possessed a masculine courage—which, alas, was afterwards put to the test—but she had a singular aptitude for such studies and knowledge as occupy men, and in which they only in general excel. On this account, besides admirably directing the education of her niece, she also conducted that of her nephew—children whom she so affectionately loved, and by whom her love was so cordially returned, that a vivid and tender shadow of those joys of motherhood she had renounced was added to the other interests with which she wisely preferred to occupy her life.

In this way nearly fifteen years glided on of regular and well-ordered existence, in which family ties, friendship, and society had each their place, but whose larger portion was reserved for seclusion and work. The villa was near enough to Naples to allow of visiting the sisters with ease, and every once or twice a-week the chief part of the Neapolitan world—then the most brilliant society to be met with in Italy—gathered about them. On other days their doors were closed. Their time then was spent in painting, study, music—for which both sisters had a gift such as amateurs rarely possess, not only playing well, but composing music; and to these must be added — or rather, above the exercise of all these talents came the many good works which they carried on unostentatiously about them, and among which was one specially dear to Adelaide. This was teaching a class of poor little boys, on whom—as we shall by and by find—she lavished a store of Christian charity and knowledge. At that time she had little leisure even for her most intimate friends; but her boys were never sent away, and their days were dearer to her than those when she was surrounded by company. Still, to judge entirely of Adelaide, it would not have been enough to see her only at work; it was necessary to watch her and listen to her in society. Her mind, as I have said, was singularly quick, penetrating, and apt of comprehension. She was also gifted with a fine imagination, and possessed in an eminent degree that promptness and quicksightedness which are Neapolitan characteristics. But what may be called her ruling quality was a kindliness which seemed to make her noble powers subserve her faculty of drawing out the good that lay in others, or in turning them to good. This quality, to tell the truth, did not quite please everybody; for, according to the ideas of many people, it makes conversation insipid if you do not speak against your neighbour. Others called it *optimism;* and some again said, that without evil-speaking conversation was robbed of its chief flavour, and was merely frivolous talk. Still there were many not unworthy of this dear woman, who found delight in the calm circle she gathered round her, and much greater pleasure in those days which were reserved for special friends, and spent in sweet and unreserved intercourse.

Ah, it was sweet indeed to talk to Adelaide,

sitting on that lovely terrace which commanded the whole view of the bay—with Naples, Vesuvius, and the mountains behind them on the left; in front, the hills above Castellamare and Sorrento, whose grand and graceful line trends away to the horizon on the other side; above our heads the splendid sky, and below us the calm and sapphire sea. When the garden-gates were shut, it seemed as if the world and men were alike banished; our conversation slid easily into more unreserved topics, and Adelaide's sunny disposition did not hinder her from being also grave. At those moments real thoughts, such as one does not interchange in society, fell easily from her lips, and were communicated without difficulty to others. Such conversations remain stamped upon the memory.

I pause here for a moment to verify my recollection of one of them, and to picture Adelaide to the eye and ear, where I shall never again behold her image, nor ever be present myself.

CHAPTER IV.

I AM going back to about the year 1854, when Adelaide's life seemed to me especially privileged and happy. I had myself enjoyed, beyond what is given to most people, the happiness of sisterly friendship; but it had been followed by great sorrows, which were then still recent, and the dear but acute remembrance of the past was often the subject of our conversation. Adelaide had known and loved all those for whose loss my tears still flowed; and while she pitied me, I envied her, for neither death nor absence had ever divided her from the two sisters whom she so loved. One of them lived with her always, a part of her very life; and the other not only came every day to see her, but brought her two children, who well deserved the tender love lavished upon them. Her life, therefore, was gifted with complete family union, added to a power of enjoyment not stripped of the brightness of youth at an age when, for the greater number, youth is already a dream of the past.

"Yes, my poor friends, but when the day of separation comes?" This thought was often before me; and on this day it led me to put the following question:

"When you think of death, how do you feel?"

She replied: "Death! but there is no such thing."

Was this indeed optimism carried to absurdity, or was it a sublime truth? The following explanation will make it clear.

"Look you," she added; "I am now feeling, praying, loving, and understanding. This is the sum of my life, and will be so to the end; then it will change, and become better, but not broken short. I, my very self, shall still go on feeling, praying, loving, and understanding. This is certainly a change in my life, but not an interruption of the life. What, then, does death mean?"

"But the suffering one may have to go through before life is ended?"

She made an Italian gesture which expresses that a thing is not worth mentioning; then she said:

"We can suffer a great deal, if we do not spend time in thinking about what we are suffering, as long as this is possible; when it becomes too difficult, God helps us, and then we can bear anything."

This is a noble way of looking at the best side of suffering and death; and the words would be beautiful even in themselves, and as nothing more. But they have a far deeper signification when we find the speaker afterwards practising her brave religious theory, and proving its sincerity by her heroic patience.

"He who does not suffer in his will, does not suffer at all," is the admirable saying of Fénelon; and this is the blessed "seed of Heaven in purgatory," transforming even the sufferings of those "who are happy in the fire,"* which, in this world, works the same change in souls whose will is wholly united to God's will. Such was, if I may so call it, the *predominant colouring* of Adelaide's piety, and the special form that Christian virtue took in her, which may also be termed the most perfect of all. Her will was never separated from the will of God, and it was her personal love for Him which operated in her soul this perfect act of her will.

Although my memory may serve me faithfully as to the past, it might possibly be doubted whether I have rendered the fore-

* "Che son contenti nel fuoco." Dante, *Inferno*, c. ii.

going conversation word for word. It will be well therefore to make some extracts from Adelaide's letters, which give a better idea of her ideas and her mind than anything I could say. I think I shall be forgiven if I go back a little, and thus take in more of these extracts, and so get a fairer idea of the charm and richness of thought which they unveil.

The letters written to her niece, who was also her god-daughter,* seem to me not only to inspire admiration for the writer, but also for the child of sixteen who was worthy to receive them.

"Posilippo, Nov. 24, 1854.

"MY DEAR CHILD,—I must write to you, I must write to you, I must write to you! Now, according to Father Borghi, a word three times repeated has an incalculable power; therefore my thrice-repeated '*I must*' ought not to re-

* Adelina del Balzo, married in 1867 to the Count di Melissa, eldest son of Prince Tignatelli Stronzolli.

main barren. '*Amen, Amen, Amen, dico vobis.*' I shall write, in spite of my visitors, in spite of lessons, in spite of my—I was about to say *in spite of our Lord;* but that would not sound well, and I must express it in other words. It is this: in spite of my dear picture of our Lord, in which I am wonderfully wrapt up just now. I never did a picture which interested me more; every stroke of the brush, every line of the features, seems an act of love which brings me nearer to my sweet Jesus. Ah, how I love that look, that comforting smile, the self-forgetfulness of that dear Face, and the Hand which I have placed upon His sacred Heart! Ah, would that I could place mine there also! I think if I held it there, I should never offend Him again, that I might become a second St. Theresa! And then, away from Him, O, how cold one becomes! how easy it is to be drawn away, to slip, and even to sin! There, my dear Pussy, that is my mood while I am writing; but who knows what it may be an hour hence?

"Adelinette, I love you; and when I chat with you, I do it from the depths of my heart, which is open to you as it is to no one else. . . .

" This is my yesterday's, or rather *to-day's* letter, the 25th. In truth, to-day I am in a quite contrary, or at least altogether different mood. The Count of Syracuse has been here. He paid us a long visit, and was kind enough to say, that as he had not seen us for a long time, he came to find us out, and see how we were. No prince royal could frame a politer phrase. And accordingly we were much flattered; and my present frame of mind is *satisfied self-love*. You see how different it is from my mood of yesterday."

"Posilippo, Dec. 27.

"To-day I have thought of you, Pussy, all day. If you only knew how pleasant it is to us to share with you any pleasant reading, or whatever it may be that is beautiful, which delights ourselves! This evening I sang a beautiful air from Verdi's *Macbeth*, representing the moment when that terrible Lady Macbeth has slain Duncan, and is washing her hands to wipe away those bloody stains which will never disappear. I daresay you know the play. I tried, in singing it, to infuse something of that fierceness which Shakespeare has so well mingled with the fearless grandeur of that dreadful woman. Clotilde and I wished for you to hear and take part in our discussions upon the matter.

"During the day we read a good deal of Père Gratry, when again we called upon you, as the poor Lydian king called upon 'Solon! Solon!' It is very beautiful when Gratry describes the created trinity in the soul, as there is an uncreated Trinity in God. I long to show you this passage, that you may see it as we do. Instead of which I must go to bed."

"Posilippo, Feb. 16.

"How the weather is gone off! My dear little friend of my heart, who knows when we shall meet? and I have so much to say to you. I have begun a large sheet of paper, that I may write, if I cannot talk.

"Ever since yesterday, when I came home from seeing Ernest,* I have longed for a good chat with you. I looked at him, and thought that now he had come to the last days of childhood. One step more, and he will have entered upon his youth. Now, then, is the flower all fresh and bright; in a couple of years, or a little more, the breath of this dirty little-great world, which he must face, may have withered it up; and then how will it be with that coming fruit, which, though still unripe, bears the promise of a rich maturity, and is so feebly defended by its frail shell? You can quite understand this parable, dear Adelina. I know

* Adelina's brother.

you can; and so knowing, I add that our good God has set near this fruit a flower-stem of earlier date, clothed with rich foliage, which will shade it from the blast and from the falling rain, and, thanks to this beneficent neighbour, the fruit will ripen into all its sweetness. You may call this the fable of *The Fruit and its Leaves*, which represents Ernest and Adelina. But to fulfil this office with him, how good and venerable you must make yourself in his eyes! How thoroughly instructed you must be in religion!—without narrowness or affectation; charitable, modest, a true woman to your fingers' ends; and yet, as I should wish, with a manly courage, and even with somewhat of a manly character, without in the least encroaching on what is *ladylike*.* Strip yourself of all petty frivolities; make yourself agreeable, but, as Clotilde says, for the sake of others, and not from self-love. If you shine in society, either by the help of

---

* *Sic* in the original.

your face or your wit, your knowledge or your position, in Heaven's name do not make a show of it.* Be simple and unpretending; humble in splendour—*umile in gloria*—like your charming Duchess of R——, who is so brilliant, and never seems to think about it. We raise our hearts to this level by driving away all those feelings of self-complacency which beset the mind after any little success. They must be treated as snares of the tempter, and we must quickly humble ourselves before God; for without this we should become base creatures, deprived of grace and gifts. Every time you succeed or please in life, think of our Lord's words, when He says He will ask an account of the talents lent to His servants, and of the moment when He will say, 'Adelina, I gave you a pleasing face, capacity, and wit; what have you done with them?' You *must* be able to answer, 'Lord Jesus, I have spent

* Literally, "do not peacock yourself about it."

them to Thy honour.' For if it shall have been to grow proud upon, or to work the least harm to others, you will deserve to perish like the wicked servant. Be therefore always simple and humble,—humble with that beautiful and characteristic virtue of the Blessed Virgin, which she has for ever dignified by the words: 'He hath put down the mighty from their seat, and hath exalted the humble and meek.'

"I do not bid you study and cultivate your mind, for you are in the habit of doing this. I have not said half what I have in my mind; but I comfort myself with thinking that you are able to make out for yourself what is incumbent upon a woman who wishes to be the friend, the guide, and the safeguard of her brother."

"Posilippo, ——

"Your father says that I must date my notes; but to do that, it would be needful to know the day of the month; and all I know at this moment is, that it is somewhere between the 20th and the 30th of February, and that it is savagely cold.* Still I do not grumble at it; for, thanks to our beloved hydropathy, I—that is, *we*—walk out bravely in the wind, without taking the least harm. I thought of you last night when I could not sleep. 'For what reason?' you will ask; and I answer, 'For none at all.' I had been composing music all the evening, and the two last verses of my song kept running in my head:

> 'Troppo la terra è povera,
> Non sazia il tuo desir.'†

Then I began to make reflections upon this word *desire*, and to compare it with that other of the *will*; and to weigh the distinction. Desire, I thought, is born in the lower part of the soul, while deliberately to will is an act fulfilled in that nobler part of it by which we draw near to God, by which we *hang upon God*, as Plato says. What a difference there is in the

* *Froid de loup.* † "Earth is too poor to satisfy thy craving."

two words!—and how this *desire* of good, which springs solely from the feeling that earth is too poor to satisfy us, fades in our eyes on deeper reflection; whilst to *will* the utmost good is indeed to become like to our Heavenly Father, and forms that perfect act to which God hearkens, and which He immediately satisfies! In this way I wandered through the realms of spirit last night, and thought of you, with whom I have so much sympathy of mind. I felt as if we were talking together, discussing the words which served us as starting-points, and thence soaring to higher thoughts. I know you like these airy flights, these wanderings into intellectual regions. How well one can discern distinctions by comparison, and perceive the various heights they contain! I told you before what Père Gratry said about the created trinity of the soul.

"How pleasantly we might spend our time together this summer! There is no one to whom I so develop my thoughts and feelings as with you, my dear girl. We understand one another so well. Whether we talk about art, literature, or more abstruse things, I should almost say that our minds are identical, if the mind of a woman of fifty could ever be like that of a girl of sixteen. But think of the almond-tree, which will be budding in a few days. When it flowers, it will be like my Adelina; later on, the rough shell will be the image of her old aunt. In the end, when the fruit ripens, it will be both flower and shell which have brought forth the almond."*

"Posilippo, May 24.

"If you only knew what pleasure your letters give me! My heart-felt joy has brought about the same sickness as befell the builders of the Tower of Babel—the confusion of tongues. Look

* The pretty playfulness of this expression is utterly lost in the translation. "La fleur et l'écorce auront toutes les deux produit l'*amende*," amande—"would have wrought amends."
Translator.

at the date of my letter, dear little one, and you will see what I have done in my hurry to answer yours.* The Marchioness de R—— and the Spanish minister are just gone. They breakfasted here; and from one subject to another, we have got on to the unimaginable time of a quarter to four. They are both extremely clever, and conversation flowed abundantly and without effort. Whenever I am so amused, I think of you; I wish you to be here, and to share everything that interests me. What weather it is now! what a day! The sea, as well as the sky, is shining with light. It ought to be like this these Whitsuntide days. Though the emotions of the soul are far above the feelings, still I am flesh and blood; and it is delightful to experience through the senses the divine effect of earthly light, when my mind is carried away by the glorious *Lux beatissima* that fills all hearts. This morning I said the

* There is a want of clearness in the text. *Translator.*

Veni, Sancte Spiritus,
Et emitte cælitus
Lucis Tuæ radium,

with the great horizon of Posilippo, in the full blaze of the sun, straight before my eyes. Ah, I can tell you it was good, both for soul and body! I write, Pussy, because I love to talk it all out to you, and it is impossible to do this when we are in the midst of people. I find very few of them ready for *psychological effusions*. However, I hope to see you this evening. My heart, which tells no falsehood, says I shall."

"Posilippo, June 12.

"'Write to me, write to me!' This is what you said in bidding me good-bye yesterday. I think you meant, 'Write me all that you did not say when they came to look for me in the garden.' Is not this what you intended to convey? As I think this a good guess, I shall go on with the meditation upon Christian doctrine, which formed the subject of our talk when we were interrupted by returning to the drawing-room. First, however, I must tell you how I enjoyed myself in your Aunt Judith's tent.* Those charming young women so beautifully dressed, the bright garden so well kept, the profusion of flowers, the lamps, the ices, our pleasant hosts, and the grace with which they did the honours, were all what they ought to have been, and pleased me much. I amused myself extremely. And now we will go back to the chief subject; but I should like to do this in Italian, for I have to explain the Catechism in that language to the boys who are good enough to come and listen to me, and do what I advise them; and it would be translating uselessly if I said the same things to you in another language. Over and above this, dear Pussy, please to pay attention to the subject, and not to the words, which I should not like to be dressing-up for you."

* The Marchioness de Sainte-Silvano. Here is added, "That is a pun;" which is omitted, because the pun vanishes in English: "*sous la tente de ta tante Judith.*"

CHAPTER V.

ANY one can judge, by the preceding extracts, how a stranger who had never lived in France, and scarcely ever visited that country, had mastered our language. She spoke Spanish even better than French; and as it had been her mother's native language, she loved it, and looked upon it as her mother-tongue. But whenever she wished to follow up continuously any deep or elevated subject, she preferred making use of Italian, which she wrote to perfection, and spoke with a purity of accent rarely met with, even in the best society, in the southern provinces of Italy. The whole of the following, and in my opinion the most remarkable portion of this correspondence, is translated from the Italian:

"I always begin my instruction by a prayer to the Holy Ghost. I ask of Him, first, understanding for those about to listen to me, that my words may be useful to them. For myself I ask for fortitude, knowledge, and counsel, as I am about to venture to explain God's word. We then all make the sign of the Cross together, and I begin. My first explanation is directed towards making the scholars understand that the Ten Commandments, which are the hinge of our whole faith, were given to men by God, that God Himself made them over to Moses engraved on stone, that they might for ever remain graven and kept in our hearts, as in perfectly pure shrines.

The first Commandment enjoins us to love God above all things; how must we live so as to fulfil this Commandment? There are three conditions:

1. The mind and body, which together form

our being, must unite to make that act of worship we all owe to our Creator.

2. God must be loved above all visible and invisible creatures.

3. God must be loved with faith, with charity, and with hope. How must we make use of the mind and body to fulfil the commandment to love God?

The mind worships God by being raised up towards Him, being occupied with Him, by calling upon Him, thanking Him, making known its wants.

The body, by bowing itself down, bending the knees, looking reverently at holy things, kissing reverently things blessed by the Church. The mind, by restraining its wandering thoughts, putting a curb on the imagination, driving away the images produced by levity or passion, and firmly directing all the powers of the soul towards God.

The body, by the mastery over the eye:ly can

and tongue; mortifying them so that each one remains externally submissive to the law of God. Laughter must not be violent or imprudent; grief must not be immoderate; tenderness must not be manifested without measure; admiration must not go to excess, &c. This is to love God with the mind and body.

My Adelina, before going further, I should like you to make a meditation upon all this. I get my boys to do so in the following way: After morning or night-prayers I give them the point I have explained to meditate upon, that they may go over and over it again, and beg of our Saviour and His sweet Mother to help them to fulfil this first part of the first Commandment. To-morrow, if you like, and if I have time, and you patience, to read and meditate afterwards, we will pass on to the second part. If you think that it does you no good, and that you know and understand all already, tell me so without hesitation, I shall thank you for your straightforwardness. I have but one object—to be of use to my god-daughter. St. John has made this a duty for me, and my love for you renders it a pleasure. Good-bye, then, my dear little angel. Love your godmother, aunt, friend, and mother, Ada."

"Posilippo, June 14, 1858.

"MY DEAR CHILD,—Supposing your yesterday's meditation made, I will put another before you: What we have to do is to love God above all things. To be sure that you love Him thus above all created things, compare in meditation the love you bear Him with the love you feel for other things that you care about the most. Would you sacrifice cheerfully the good health you enjoy, to gain the love of God? Would you spend the whole of your life in bed, to cling to God's will? Would His love make up to you for so sad a state? Think well over this, meditate well upon it, put yourself in this situation, and see if you feel within you the strength to sacrifice your health to God. If you really can attain to the interior acceptance of such a martyrdom, God will accept this holocaust in Heaven, and bless you just as if you effectually and truly suffered it for His sake. But you must well understand, my Joy [*Gioja mia*], that you must not make this a lip-offering. Vain words satisfy men, but not God. If your offering is made *truly* from the bottom of your heart, as if the sacrifice were there ready to fulfil, the offering will be reckoned to you in God's sight, and you will have the merit of it for ever. As you have done in regard to your health, so apply the sacrifice to other things that you prize. Would you give up your birth and position in the world for love of God? Life, honour? Would you be judged other than what you are—deceitful, false, and mean? Would you bear to see every one dear to you taken from you one after the other, while you stand face to face with God, who has thus stript you? And would you give them all up, rather than offend His love?

"If, indeed, you feel able to renounce everything in this way for Him, you can say with truth that you love God above all things. But as 'to will and to do' are not the same to us, beg of our Saviour and His Blessed Mother the strength which is wanting to put your thoughts into practice. Of ourselves we can do so little; but with God's help the impossible becomes possible. I will not enlarge upon this. Meditate with God's help, and pray for your godmother and friend, Ada."

"June 15.

"MY DEAR GODDAUGHTER,—We must love God with faith. Try, therefore, to reckon up the ways in which we may fail in this duty, and you will then avoid the occasions of this grave offence. For instance, we sin against faith by believing in superstitions. Many otherwise sensible people are subject to this absurd defect, which ought only to attach to the narrowest minds.

In this category must be placed such mischievous superstitions as the evil eye, casting a blight upon any object, bad luck on Fridays, spilling salt and oil, dining thirteen at table; and many other inconceivable superstitions, with which we are flooded to such a degree that, as I say, we meet with well-educated, sensible, and even pious people, who are not ashamed to give in to a faultiness which is not only offensive to God, but even sins against natural reason and plain good sense. I know that you are not given to this pettiness; but we must watch against it. There comes a time when the human mind declines with age, and seems to return to its first childhood; when the bold become wary, and the wary timid; when the large and open heart narrows, and the natural activity languishes. We must therefore bear in mind this deterioration of age, and strengthen those weak places which are most liable to decay. Fly from all superstition in youth, arm yourself with religious strength and holy reason, and you will never fall into it."

"Posilippo, June 27.

"MY DEAR LITTLE CHILD,—Another way of offending God's love, is not to obey His holy law; for love dictated this law, and by despising it, we despise the love that imposed it. To infringe the Divine law, is a sin which disturbs the order of creation, and the harmony of its great whole. We are too imperfect to understand the vastness of the material and intellectual worlds; the uncreated and Almighty Creator alone can understand and contain them; consequently He alone can impose upon all the component parts of His creation the laws they are to follow. It is possible to understand approximately this truth by applying it to a machine invented by human intelligence. Take, for instance, a pianoforte. The ingenious workman who made it has subjected each of the parts composing it to some particular law. The keys on which we place our fingers lift the hammers, the hammers strike the wires, the leathers which cover the hammers deaden the blows; and thus each detail is contrived, and follows the law fixed by the contriver. Tell me, Adelina, what would be the consequence if the keys did not lift the hammers which strike the wires, or if the wires obstinately refused to vibrate under the blows received? In this case what would become of the instrument contrived with such care and intelligence? Would it not become a mere mass of useless fragments which have ceased to form an instrument? What would the artisan, who ought to love his work, do in this case? Would he not burn every refractory piece of it, or oblige them altogether to follow their first laws? Thus God, who loves His work, and sees it disturbed by the rebellion of some one of the souls He has created, requires that rebellious soul to return to the law of order, which is the law of love."

"Posilippo, July 2.*

"To-day I shall leave you without any meditation. It is good for you to rest, and it is not bad that I should rest a little too. Let us, then, leave Sinai, child of my heart, and let us climb Mount Parnassus. There too we shall have light from above, but with a difference; for on the summit of the holy mount we are in the centre of the great fire of charity, whilst on Parnassus we only find one of its beams, which is Beauty. But it is the self-same light, as you acknowledge, do you not? Come, let us climb together to the peak, where we can gather the laurel; and before we get so far I shall leave you to the care of your Muse,—*Erato*, I think,—not being able to mount so high. There is a region which I cannot go beyond; but I will be your Virgil so far, and will even give you some advice before trusting you to the care of that Beatrice who will lead

* This letter is in French.

you to the upper heights. This is my first advice. You wish to compose verses to set to music; try therefore to bring into your verses some phrase expressing the leading idea you want to convey. All the words that are set to a melody do not reach the listener's ear; some are inevitably lost in the air, which then takes the first place with the audience. To communicate your intention, therefore, to other minds, some predominant word is necessary, which disposes them to understand what the music expresses. Let me see if I cannot better explain my idea by an example. For instance, here is one. Azioli composed a piece of eight or ten verses, the first of which begins, *Solitudine campestre, &c.** After which the poetry says a thousand things that one does not enter into; but these words suffice to convey the leading idea, and, after they have struck the ear, it is impossible to expect a tarantella or

---

* "Ye woodland solitudes," &c.

a march. Again, supposing verses, in which the word *anathema* occurs, preceded and followed by such as express *who* is anathematised, and all the circumstances of the time, the place, and the persons pertaining to the situation,—the key-note of the music is the word *anathema*, which contains the principal idea. Do you understand this? And now here I am at the end of my tether. Follow your Muse, and climb to the mountain top.

"After you went away yesterday, Monsignor Ferrieri* stayed some time, and we were sorry that you were not here when he enumerated the qualities which he thinks ought always to characterise a Papal Nuncio. 'The sacred character of the priest,' he said, 'should always prevail above that of the diplomatist. Straightforwardness and loyalty should be his two principal virtues; for if he serves the State, he should never forget that it is the Pope whom he repre-

* Papal Nuncio at Naples.

sents.' He was admirable upon this and several other subjects, and interested us very much."

"Posilippo, July 12.

"The voice from Sinai has been a long time silent. Moses sleeps, and I am dumb; but this morning, while I was getting up, the third Commandment seemed to resound in my ears, and I now begin again, or continue my meditations: 'Keep holy the Sabbath-day.' In hearing these words, it seems to me that they are a counsel to Martha to cut short her activity, and to Mary to redouble her prayers. *Servite Dominum in lætitia*, says the Psalmist. Let us serve the Lord with gladness, and make a good and cheerful use of those created things He gives us to use."

"July 20.

"I delayed going on, because the subject is difficult for my small understanding and briefer knowledge. But I should like to do my best to fulfil my duty towards you, my darling god-daughter. All the Masses that have been celebrated since our Lord's time till now, and all those that will be celebrated till the Last Day, are *only one Mass*. The multitude of priests is but one priest. The Victim is one, the Sacrifice is one; for Christ being both Priest and Victim, and He being infinite and eternal, the sacrifice, priest, and victim can be but one and lasting. Tomaso Rossi, the great theologian and philosopher, makes a beautiful comparison on this subject, explaining remarkably well the unity and multiplicity of the Holy Sacrifice of the Mass. He says that one articulate sound, expressing an idea by means of the human voice, is one and simple when it leaves the mouth of the speaker, but becomes multiplied indefinitely in the air by the sounds which, with perfect likeness of form and substance, strike the surrounding multitude. This is the result of a natural cause, by which unity is multiplied without division. Let us apply this thought to the Word Incarnate, and the Sacrifice of the Cross He once offered for us; that sacrifice which, without ceasing to be one, is multiplied by the numberless sacrifices offered upon the Altar, which all of them, everywhere and for ever, communicate to each one of the faithful the effects and merit of the first and only sacrifice of Christ. When, therefore, we assist at Mass, we do not assist at a *representation* of the sacrifice of Calvary, but at that sacrifice itself, which is *enduring*. Oh, if we could imbue our minds thoroughly with this great truth, with what devotion we should assist at the holy, most holy, Sacrifice of Mass!

"I am almost afraid to write to you on such a subject; and I earnestly beg of the Holy Spirit, to Whom always I commend myself in these cases, to suggest to me terms which shall be exact, and not too unworthy for what I strive to convey to you on these high and solemn subjects."

"Posilippo, Sept. 9, 1858.

"We are not the least troubled at finding you somewhat occupied with the positive matters of life; for we must not forget that we walk upon this earth. No doubt, during our brief stay here, we are permitted sometimes to fly like birds to recreate ourselves, and to rise to a greater or lower height on the wings of science, literature, or art, and to stay more or less time in those airy regions at which we are allowed to glance, but in which we may not stay. Sooner or later we must return to our place in this great slough, to which we are bound by Adam's sin. Let us, then, learn to explore our place of banishment, and try to draw out of it the greatest good we can; and, with this aim, let us make some inquiries into the positive and material side of our being. I hope that a commendation thus expressed will not lead you to suppose that I wish to see you plunged into this same morass. No, no. Give part of your mind to calculation and reasoning; part of your intellectual faculties to the world; but keep the best and highest part of your being for God. Mount upwards to Him on the wings of His love; nothing wearies them, and they bear us into realms which it is not only permitted us to explore, but *to dwell in*, since the Almighty Himself sustains us there.

"Special occupations have a very good side, and we have always, too, some marked tendency towards one thing or another. But to like one way only, is the sign of a narrow mind, for the understanding of man is very rich; and if we obstinately persist in receiving through one source of the mind what has to be given out and spread through many various channels, we impoverish the mind as well as ourselves. We must simply discern and observe, and try to extract for ourselves all the good that each subject contains. We are surrounded here, even in our limited society, by people who differ much from one another. Some are bent towards serious subjects, others disposed for philosophical speculation; the greater part devoted to the frivolities of daily life. Some few privileged souls soar to the heights, and relish poetry and loftier subjects. Finally, at the end of all, come the train of people devoted to specialties, and who are grubbing in them from morning till night, and from night till morning."

CHAPTER VI.

AMONG all these extracts, which I think will not be found fault with for their length—extracts so varied, and upon such different topics, in which Adelaide's elevated tone, charming character, and beautiful mind are clearly shown—there is one special passage which cannot be read without emotion, when we bear in mind the trial which awaited her at the end of life. It is that where she begs her youthful correspondent to set before her, and accept beforehand, for the love of God, every imaginable suffering. In examining her expressions at that moment, one sees how she had long since strengthened her mind and aroused her own courage; and the efficacy of this means, proved later by the result, is enough to induce the weak to become strong, and the fearful brave. But at the time when she thus spoke of suffering as one of the possible chances of the future, she was already enduring it; and from that moment she practised the acceptance of suffering for the love of God with a perfection which would have been more perceptible if she had appeared conscious of it herself. In consequence of a serious fall some years before, she had been subject to continual discomfort, and walked lame and with difficulty. This sudden interruption to her natural activity, and the sharp pains which sometimes attacked her, would have been considered by another as a sufficient trial; but she dwelt upon these things so little, that in the end she managed to make them forgotten by others; and in this way the years slipped away till 1863, when an event, which at first sight would seem not likely to produce such consequences, brought about an unexpected change in the sisters' peaceful life. By some rare accident in Italy, the part of the

Strada Nuova in which their villa stood was entirely destitute of any church, and the only chapel to which they had access was at too great a distance for walking, especially for Adelaide. This circumstance, which was simply an annoyance and a hindrance to her, was a far more real and serious evil to the surrounding population. The people neglected their religious practices from the impossibility of attending to them, and by little and little their piety decayed. Struck and grieved by what had come about, the two sisters formed the plan of building in this district, not a small chapel merely for their own use, but a real church, which should benefit the whole neighbourhood. "Deeds, not words," might well be looked upon as their motto; and it rarely happened in their case that a good thought did not become a good action, if their strong will could bring it about. They chose for the site of their plan a spot called Bellavista, not far from their own house; and having obtained from the munificence of Francis II. a small grant of land, they set themselves to work without seeking farther aid. They got a plan after their own taste from Germany, which departed widely from the false Greek and still falser Renaissance styles generally in vogue in Naples; and then, almost without an architect, and with only the workmen, whom they overlooked themselves, aided by their own understanding, persistence, and self-denial, in four years' time the church was built and opened to the public. Thanks to the zeal of two excellent and admirable priests, whose help they secured, this church became a central fire, whence the faith and piety of the neighbourhood, which had died out only for want of support, was rekindled. Two wings, ending in two towers, were added to the church: one intended as a school and refuge for the poor; while the other was divided into small rooms, the letting of which might, to a certain extent, cover some of the considerable expense incurred in carrying out this charitable work. Still, as so often happens in such cases, the expenses exceeded what had been intended, and the good work they had carried out obliged the generous sisters to make greater sacrifices than they had anticipated. It ended in their going to occupy the wing-tower of the church themselves, and in their giving up their charming villa at Posilippo—the chosen and beloved retreat in which they had intended to live and die. They left it immediately and for always, apparently even without regret, so unmurmuring was their act. This was the sacrifice they offered, calmly pursuing and attaining their object of doing the utmost amount of good to the greatest possible number.

I can here appeal to the recollection of all who knew them at that time; and they will not gainsay me while I testify that this fruitful good work, destined to insure the well-being of the surrounding population, as much as their religious practice, was carried out almost in silence, and with such simplicity that very few even of the most frequent visitors at the elegant villa of Posilippo knew why it had been exchanged for another home. Some, indeed, went so far as to accuse the sisters of whim and imprudence; others expressed their wonder at their fancy of building a church, and pulled its architecture to pieces. But no one paused to weigh the extent of their sacrifice, or thought of asking the reasons for making it, any more than the sisters did of rendering an explanation of their deeds.

These recollections, I must own, suggest comparisons which are not without sorrow and shame. My memory depicts afar off, in the midst of the wealth and splendour of Paris, a poor shabby little chapel, not even sufficing for the devotion of those who frequent it, much less providing for the wants of those who cannot find room in it. The need of a church in this district, or at least of a larger chapel, is felt by every one; and yet there is no one who thinks of silently sacrificing a portion of his goods to carry out this much-needed and desirable work. I repeat it with shame, there cannot be found in that opulent neighbourhood wealth enough to carry out what two generous women did unaided, without noise or display, at Naples.

By a curious chance, when Adelaide Minutolo came to Paris in her hour of trial, she was lodging close to the little chapel I am speaking of, and often went into it to pray. Probably she observed its poverty with surprise, and contrasted it with what the splendour of the neighbouring quarter might lead one to expect. But I can certainly undertake to say, that such reflections as I have just been making never occurred to her mind; and that she had no more idea of complacency in her own acts than on the day when, yielding to the necessity so generously and freely imposed upon herself, she left her beloved home for ever.

CHAPTER VII.

WHILST the church and turrets of Bellavista were rising from the foundations, serious events were succeeding one another in Italy, and Naples especially had gone through a violent, rapid, and radical change. What impression had they made upon Adelaide's noble character? what had been the feelings of her religious heart, and the thoughts of her steadfast and manly mind? These things must be told; for the picture I am drawing of her would be unfinished, if I either suppressed or changed a single feature. And it must also be remembered, and we must never seek to deny it, that when, early in 1859, the words *power, independence,* and *liberty* were uttered for the first time, they caused all hearts to beat quickly. Some sudden vision appeared of a country waited for, beloved, craved for, but never possessed; and this rapid thrill of feeling was experienced by a large number of good and fervent Catholics, no less than by those who so promptly arrayed themselves on the enemy's side. But when that day came — alas, too speedily! — when blinded and ungrateful Italy grasped with violent hands the property of the Church, uplifting her impious voice against its august Head, and making arrogant pretensions upon Rome, it was these very people who suffered most of all.

I may almost say, that they were the only sufferers; for the partisans on the other side, to whom the excesses and mistakes of their country were a boon, took advantage of those very excesses and mistakes to reap a harvest for themselves. I venture, therefore, to repeat, that the Italians who suffered with truly bleeding hearts were those who, while loving their country, and sharing many of its aspirations, loved their faith, their Church, and their God a thousand times more, and were now forced to know, with unspeakable anguish of soul, that an impassable barrier had sprung up between the two affections which are the sweetest and most desirable to unite. And in this way Adelaide also felt, discerned, and suffered.

Still, it was not in her character to give way to dejection and discouragement, and she hoped, in spite of everything, to the end—hoped, perhaps, under delusion, but with passionate desire, that a day would come for Italy when these two affections might meet in the same heart—a day when, pausing upon the fatal precipice, awakened from a fascination unworthy of all her recollections, and destructive of all her hopes, Italy should open her eyes clearly to her grand mission and true office; should bow down with joy and with *pride*, if the word were a fitting one for repentance, before *that holy spot where the successor of the great Peter sets his chair;** and thus should deserve that blessing, and with the blessing its peace :

"From those fatherly hands whence blessing comes."†

* " Lo loco santo,
U' siede il successor del maggior Piero."
Dante.

† " De ces mains paternelles d'où le pardon descend."
V. Hugo.

CHAPTER VIII.

THIS was, in brief, the state of Adelaide's mind at this difficult and painful juncture; and it was not satisfactory either to the exclusive defenders of a past time, or to the excited partisans of the future—to these last perhaps less than to the former; for while entering into all that was lofty and generous — perhaps we might say ideal—in their love for their country, she never ceased to show a personal, keen, and respectful affection to the princes whom the changes in Italy had overthrown. Whether right or wrong, she discerned in the transformation undergone by her country the plans of Providence; she lent faith to such changes, but grieved over the losses which ensued from them; she loved those whose high position obliged them to suffer, and lost no opportunity of testifying without fear her esteem and regret. Once, among other occasions, she sent a bouquet of flowers to the young Queen,* whose crown had fallen almost before it had been placed upon her head. This act was blamed by the more violent of both sides; but those to whom the reverence was paid—more generous than either their adherents or their enemies—understood and accepted it, and later on, welcomed the giver with a goodness at once honourable to themselves and to her. This time also neither their graciousness nor the act which called it forth was well received by all. In history there are days when nothing but violence seems to make itself heard; as during a storm nothing less noisy than itself is observed. But when time shall have rolled on, and the stormy days we are passing through shall have gone by; when the hatred they have engendered shall be extinct, the face of things will be changed, and

* Of Naples.

we shall be better able to judge of those who maintained their mutual affection and esteem throughout the heat of the struggle; and above all, of those who, mastering the bitterness of their reverses, still preserved their sense of justice, and never confounded the opponents divided from them by disinterested and sincere conviction, with the crowd of traitors and base men who advocate every revolution, and are always the worshippers of success. When this day of peace and moderation shall have dawned — though scarcely, alas! in our time — then Adelaide's withered nosegay will be not only a relic, but a symbol also.

CHAPTER IX.

AMONG all the chords—some of them contradictory—which vibrated at the same time in Adelaide's heart, there was one which sounded with more remarkable and characteristic strength there than elsewhere, in a country where individual and disinterested action is more rarely to be met with than in others. It may seem strange, but it is true, that the motto, " Each one's deed is the saving of all," is better understood in Italy by women than by men. Be that as it may, Adelaide's noble heart was now filled with the desire of making some effort, some sacrifice, or act of personal devotion for the common good. It seemed to her that, as, after an earthquake, the more fearless look about them, not for a shelter for themselves, but to see to whom they can stretch out a hand, so in this great national shock which caused the whole earth to tremble, instead of seeking her own security or ease, it was needful to see what advantage zeal, courage, and faith could take of the words *liberty*, *reform*, and *progress*, which, if sincerely believed in, invite large-hearted men to put their hands to the work. But, in truth, the rule under which Naples had lived was in no way suited for the development of energy. We know that limbs long bound and stiffened have not, when first set free, any great vigour in moving, and this fact seemed to impose upon the more energetic the duty of acting without waiting for others. This was Adelaide's opinion, and the motive which made her accept, for a while, the hardest of all sacrifices. She still believed that it was not necessary to break up the monuments of the past, but to restore them; that it was possible rather to heal than to open the wounds of her country, to create rather than to sweep away; and she offered herself for the work. She was willing to forego her sweet and beloved retirement, her peaceful and occupied life, her daily intercourse with friends; and all to devote herself to a difficult, dangerous, thankless, and we may as well say at once hopeless, undertaking, which after a few months she was obliged to give up.* Adelaide's belief in the goodness of others had hindered her from perceiving how her very singleness of will, the purity of her desire for progress—by which she meant the only true advance—and her refined and delicate feelings, —how, in fact, the exquisite qualities she possessed, left her standing alone in a task in which, above all, she required to be seconded. She found it therefore very soon beyond her strength —already touched by the secret approach of the fatal malady soon about to reveal itself.

* This was, the superintendence and reform of a celebrated institution, into which, for many years, serious abuses had crept.

She quietly withdrew from it, and returned to the solitude which she never left again, having reaped some sad experience during this brief appearance in a region troubled by the world's intrigues—experience most especially sad to one whose mind never willingly opened to anything but good-will, and who liked ever to shut her eyes to that aspect of human nature which is always contemptible if we look at it too closely.

At this time, if any bitterness dwelt in her heart, she might have had some pretext for showing or expressing it; but there was none to be found. She wished well to the most unjust and the most thankless. One day, a few steps from her, Adelaide saw two people mimicking her tottering walk, speaking of her the while with malevolence and contempt. She only smiled her sweet smile; and we are certain of telling the truth when we say, that if she could have done anything at that moment for her insulters, she would have done it gladly and with ease; for self-love found no dwelling on the heights which in that soul were bathed with Divine goodness. Not a trace of pain remained in her mind after an event which might have troubled the calm of her soul so much the more on account of the great tranquillity of her life.

Having returned to her seclusion, Adelaide took up again, with greater industry than ever, her former habits, and, as before, her time was spent between work, study, and charities, whose opportunities, having become almost infinitely multiplied in a revolutionary time, took all forms; and this is why, we may say in passing, those who love their country, on whichever side, should never avoid the opportunities of charity at such a time. God and the Guardian Angels of Bellavista alone know all that was done there during those years, whose storms are not yet assuaged, and what good works followed her who was so soon to be called before the Sovereign Judge to receive her reward.

In that near neighbourhood of the town the principal houses are only occupied by inmates who remain there for a short time, and during the heat of the summer, when it is preferable to enjoy the beauty of the views from a distance, and under the fresh shelter of the terraces and balconies—*loggie*—than in traversing on foot the steep and sandy ways which lead to the dwellings of the poor. It follows, therefore, that the numerous, wretched, and scattered populace is less civilised, less known, and worse helped than others in Naples who are much more centrally remote, but in the neighbourhood of better sources of assistance. All these poor had now, thanks to the Church of Bellavista and its charitable neighbours, a centre round which they could gather with cheerful joy. Their gratitude on the one hand, and on the other the reasonable influence exerted by energy of character, joined to a large and kindly heart, such as Adelaide's, had created real bonds between herself and her poor neighbours. It is not possible to relate here the number of pious, wise, and useful ways in which this influence was exercised; but we will point out one, among others, which often arose from the new and troubled state of Italy, and specially of the Neapolitan states. It often came to pass that men who could not avoid the conscription, now more rigidly enforced than formerly, endeavoured to make their escape. Several of these men, who were hiding in the neighbourhood of Bellavista, were brought down by want to implore charity of Adelaide. Her charity never failed them; but while her hand was opened to help, her gentle voice exhorted them to return to their allegiance, and almost always sent back, submissive and contented to their standards, men whom the habit of lawless living would soon have led to violate all law, not as discontented citizens, but as criminals.

Days thus occupied were often concluded, as

formerly, by evenings given to their relations and friends. The drawing-room in the Bellavista tower became no less peopled than that at Posilippo, and the new home had become nearly as dear to Adelaide as the old. Never, probably, had the sweet and lofty interests of her existence been more numerous or more keenly felt; and never had that existence been more valued by her family, or more useful to all with whom she had to do.

It was at that very time, unknown to every one, that a disease which had sprung up without seeming of any importance—a tumour, at first scarcely visible, in the lower part of the right cheek—began to assume some importance from the pain, which almost immediately made her suspect and dread the cause. To those who accompanied her, indeed, on that long way of the Cross, which was to lead her to eternal life, it is impossible to doubt that she had, from the first, discerned and firmly faced the danger which threatened her. The first shot, it is said, makes the bravest man wince; and those who grow the best accustomed to war confess that they stoop their heads at the first bullet which whistles by their ears. If, therefore, Adelaide was for an instant disturbed by the early appearance of such a danger, it would only be natural, and no reflection on her courage; but nothing of the kind took place. What passed between God and her soul we do not know, though the end may reveal to us somewhat; but we keep the remembrance engraven on our minds of the empire which she maintained over herself, of her unchanged evenness of temper, her brave and unalterable cheerfulness and perfect freedom of spirit; and find traces of these qualities in all the letters she wrote at that time, from which we shall give several extracts. They are written in Italian, having been addressed to the Marchioness of Sonora, her eldest sister; and the first was sent off at the time when

Adelaide felt the earliest symptoms of her fatal malady, then aggravated by a painful attack of erysipelas.

CHAPTER X.

"Oct. 14.

"NO, my Pauline, we cannot go to San Prisco on Monday. That little swelling on my cheek 'mounts towards the meridian of its life,'* and goes on *crescendo* every day with a fine whimsical effect, that, according to the rules of Fabio Pallavicini, somewhat disturbs the symmetry of my face; but in the matter of outline, beauty is relative, and every one has his own taste. For my part, this little *Berninesque* tendency does not disturb me."

"Oct. 17.

"The first thing I have to tell you to-day, Pauline, is that my cheek grows in beauty, and at this moment is of the most splendid red. It may be I could wish this erysipelas to be less

* "Sale l' arco della sua vita." *Dante.*

sharp; but if it tortures me, it will not be for long; for the vigour of its constitution cannot, they say, outlive nine days; after which, whether it chooses or not, it will be obliged to grow less, and finally lose itself *in the nothingness to which all creation hastens.**

"Mesdames Pzennyfass and Giroux have invited us to inspect the fashions they have received from Paris. I have sent to get two crinolines, which will give us the circumference of the comet—save its tail, which, they say, is 12,000,000 miles long. O, how ill this erysipelas makes me! How can one write wittily when the treacherous body will oblige one to think of it, whether or not? In spite of this, I should like, as they say in Spain, '*de tripas corazon*,' that is, cause the strength of my soul to pass into my body. Yes, the soul, that noble lady, shall be uppermost, and shall subdue her slave! There, I think that sentence already

* " Nel nulla ove corre tutto il creato." *Dante.*

rings with a little spiritual strength! What do you say? Come, victory!"

This accidental malady, of which she so brightly complains, was overcome; and Adelaide's friends, glad to encourage one another, thought her cured, and ceased to think of infirmities which she never mentioned, and of which nothing either in her face or general health made them suspect the serious nature. In the course of the autumn, Adelaide and her sister went away for some weeks into the neighbourhood of Naples; and she gives an account of their visit to her elder sister in the following letter:

"Castellamare, Thursday.

"Everything was ready for our departure the other day, when the idea suddenly occurred to us to change our route; which idea we carried out with a promptness and capacity equal to Napoleon's when he changed the plan of his campaign upon a drum-head. Instead of attacking first the gorges of La Cava, we suddenly fell upon Sorrento, which we occupied for four-and-twenty hours. After making sure of that point, we scaled without opposition the pass of Scutari, and in two hours' time gained the heights of Castellamare, where we found a division of cavalry and infantry, by whose help we attained the finest spot in the neighbourhood. There, under dear Zeneide's* hospitable roof, we pitched our tent; and this will be our head-quarters till the end of October.

"Our booty at Sorrento is wholly composed of holy matters, the greater part of which I have planted deep down in my heart, where I hope they will take root. But what I should like to make known to the public is a very beautiful discussion I have had with Babet Fonton† on the subject of the Immaculate Conception; a discussion upon which you will

---

* The Countess of Lebzeltone.
† Mademoiselle Elizabeth Fonton.

be allowed to decide. Moreover I should tell you that I have added to our Lady's Litany one more invocation: 'Holy Shrine of Christ, pray for us.'*

"At Castellamare our spoils have been of a more worldly sort, but yet not wholly frivolous. The intellectual portion was made up of several conversations, parti-coloured—*vario-pinti*—as well as by a historical course, collected in the live walking book called Mons. du Pach, and also the beautiful melody of the poem Campagna† is writing, which he gives us in morsels that are immensely charming.

---

* "*Theca sancta Christi, ora pro nobis.*"

† Giuseppe Campagna, whose poems, which are justly valued in his own country, have been published in several portions, but always incomplete, and with an indifference as to their success, which in Italy chiefly characterises those who deserve it. The poem of which Adelaide Minutolo speaks here is still partly unpublished, and is called *L'Abate Gioacchino*, containing beautiful passages, which make it desirable to publish it entire. Giuseppe Campagna was suddenly carried off less than a year ago; a loss to his country, his family, and to literature, as well as to the numerous friends he had made in France, where he spent the latter years of his life.

"From Du Pach's gossip I have gleaned that Marie-Antoinette was of a middle size when you saw her in her morning-gown, but in public she wore high-heeled shoes, which, added to her royal way of carrying her head, gave her the appearance of being very tall. It was thought that she had red hair, because her skin was so extremely fair, and her eyebrows were of that colour. He said *it was thought*, because in her day the horrible fashion of powder made a mystery of the real colour of the hair.

"As to Campagna's poem, the first part is far advanced. Eugenio beholds the figure representing Humanity scourged by *Progress*, who drives him on, while the evil spirit *Standstill—statu quo*—holds him back, and after gazing into the gulf behind him, he looks up towards the cloud-capped mountains, to which he tends. .... What an idea, to attempt to tell you a poem in prose! Enough; but let me tell you, I admire it, and think it full of beauty."

"Dec. 6.

"Alas, it is too true! The poor Count of Syracuse is dead. In spite of his faults, his mistakes, and his misdoings, he was a remarkable prince, and one who, in other times perhaps, might have been lauded to the skies. It is a misfortune to men, and specially to princes, that they may never enjoy their own historical reputation. Their little faults, when seen on a near view, tarnish their splendid qualities; and if there be any moral defect, we dare not praise them, lest we should be too indulgent to what is beautiful when severed from what is good. Poor Count of Syracuse! He will be, nevertheless, mourned by many, and sincerely regretted by a few, among whom I reckon myself. But while the chief part of his contemporaries will probably speak of him as a fool, who knows if posterity, looking upon what he has achieved, and calling to mind his taste for art and his patronage of science and literature—who knows whether they will not call him '*The illustrious Leopold de Bourbon*'? You are right; let us say more than one *requiem* for him; for, alas, his mind's eye, which discerned so well earthly things, was closed to the Heavenly, and this caused him to live as if this life was the end of all. Let us pray, oh, let us pray for him! It is the only means of returning the friendship he always showed us, and the kindnesses by which he did us honour. He often spoke to me of *comradeship;* but I never would accept from him the name of 'comrade.' To me he was always a prince; but now his remains and his rank are alike in the grave, I accept the title. Our souls are equal, and I am now going to pray heartily for *my brother*, while exercising the art which we both loved so well."

To Adelina.

"Mamma has no doubt spoken to you about my health, and you have heard the news of the little swelling in my cheek, which is as bright and shining as a billiard-ball; otherwise I am very well; and to-day treated myself to a morning walk to Bagnoli, with which I am much pleased. Yesterday we had a visit which troubled all three of us. We were out on the terrace after dinner, when we heard the large door-bell ring. The next minute we saw a gentleman appear with an elegant lady on his arm. It was L. and O. Oh, how changed he is! His face disfigured by that swelling, of a ghastly colour, and his eyes sunk. He dragged himself along with difficulty, but still wished to see everything; however, after a little while, his strength failed him. We took him out on the terrace, which he thought beautiful, and he looked at everything with interest. Then I carried him to my painting-room, where we sat down, and stayed talking. He looks as if he must die, not suffering acute pain, but what he calls with indescribable gentleness, 'a disagreeable continual pain,' —*un antipatico continuo dolore.* After recovering a little from the upset it gave me, I was able to chat and keep up cheerful conversation; even to say some jesting things, which diverted him, and drew him out of his sad thoughts. They went away before dark, as they were afraid of the drive in the open carriage. In taking leave he pressed my hand so earnestly, and with such continued and meaning pressure, that it fully seemed a farewell. Almost at the same moment Augustus Craven came in, and I felt very grateful for his visit, for it gradually removed the sad feelings which had been called up."

CHAPTER XI.

ALAS! the friend of whom she speaks, and to whom she had indeed bidden a last farewell, was stricken with exactly the same disease as herself, and sank under it a few months afterwards. Her way of relating this meeting seems to show how sadly it reacted on herself, which was so unusual with her as to be worth remarking, as it is nearly the only instance where it is possible to take hold of any expression of the kind either in her words or writings. She now faced the probabilities of the future without trouble or alarm; but the chief thought and object which she steadily pursued up to the day but one before her death was to spare her eldest sister as long as possible. She knew that Pauline's tender affection led her to shrink from the idea of danger, and she held tenaciously to the determination not to disturb her beforehand with anxiety. She concealed nothing from the friend who never left her; and spoke openly to some others, bravely calling the frightful disease* she dreaded by name; but spoke of it as little as possible even to them, and was always the first to draw their attention from the subject. Neither did she ever exaggerate the evil to herself; and when the means of cure were suggested to her, she accepted the hope, and made ready for the attempt with calmness and resignation.

During that autumn Adelaide liked to sit alone in the twilight, while her sister played to her on the piano, or sang songs which she had sung formerly herself, or that they had composed together. From time to time then she permitted her tears to fall,—tears of feeling, but not of sadness; for it was not sadness, but affection, which sickness was ripening in her. A greater

* Cancer.

love than ever for God; a greater affection than ever for those whom she loved on earth. She suffered from the party animosity which since the revolution, and possibly for long before, had destroyed that mutual good feeling which had been the delightful and characteristic feature of Neapolitan society, and she continually repeated to her sister: "Oh, I beg of you, now more than ever, *let us have nothing but honey upon our lips.*" These are certainly beautiful words, which in times of party warfare Christians at least should always keep in mind.

During the winter of 1865 she grew worse, and the surgeons who were called in differed in opinion. Adelaide decided, therefore, to set off with her sister to consult some one in Paris; and towards the end of May they began their journey. The tumour, and still more the sufferings it caused, were greatly increased. In crossing the Alps she felt, as I heard her afterwards very simply express it, *as if all her teeth were being pulled out.* It can scarcely be believed that notwithstanding this torture, and the sad anxieties which must have preoccupied her on such a journey, her mind was sufficiently free and her courage great enough to enjoy all the beauty of the natural scenery and of art, and to be interested in everything in that Northern Italy, which, no less than the South, she called her country. Three old friends* who were at Paris when she arrived flew to the hotel to which she had just driven, and were received with open arms, and the same smile as if the meeting had been brought about by a pleasure-trip. She answered the anxious questions put to her by saying she was come to consult Dr. Nélaton, to know decidedly what course to take. "If he says that an operation is not necessary, so much the better, and I shall go back content. If the contrary, I shall submit, but shall go back all

---

* The Marchioness de Rende, the Viscountess Des Cars, and the writer of this memoir.

the same to Naples to undergo it; for if I die, I should not like to die away from my own people."

This, in fact, was her intention before seeing Nélaton. She had to wait three days for his visit, which was perhaps the utmost trial of patience she had to bear throughout. When at last he came for his first visit, he was doubtful; and his doubt gave her friends, her sister, and herself, very great hopes. The next day he came again with another surgeon, whose experience in that special disease he thought more extensive than his own. I had not courage to look at them when they came out of the room where they had been consulting. She herself told me their decision. She must not think of going home. The operation was inevitable, and must be performed at once. I looked at her much overcome, but she was far calmer than I was. "Do not be anxious," she said; "I am not afraid." And as she kissed me, she added in a low voice, and with a tone I shall never forget, "*And I love God more than ever.*"

Four days afterwards her three friends were with Adelaide and her sister at seven o'clock in the morning. It was a lovely morning in June, the windows of the sitting-room were open, and Adelaide, brave and peaceful, was sitting at one of them, and appearing to enjoy the beauty of the weather, just as she would on any other day. She had prepared herself the day before by receiving Communion in the little chapel near, and now had nothing more to do than to put in practice that acceptance of God's will which for so many years had been her act of daily love.

A sister of *Bon-Secours* and two surgeons were there to help Dr. Nélaton; but he had decided that no one else should be present at the operation. Just before it, he thought it necessary to prepare Adelaide for the probable consequences of what she would go through; and tracing with his finger the outline of the immense incision he was about to lance, he forewarned her that she would not only remain disfigured, but that she would probably lose all movement of the right eye, as well as of one side of her mouth. This was to be the result, even if the operation was successful! It may be imagined with what feelings her poor sister and her friends heard these words; but she turned to them with the same sweet smile. "Take one good look at me once more, dear friends," she said; "for you will never behold this beautiful face again as you see it now." And having said this, she calmly left the sitting-room in which we were to remain, to enter that chamber from which none could say whether she would come forth living or dead.

The door was closed; and we stayed there waiting silently for four-and-fifty minutes! During that time not a word was uttered in our room, and not a cry, nor a sound was heard from the other, although the unconsciousness from chloroform only lasted twelve minutes. All the rest of the time she had felt and suffered everything. Afterwards she told us that when she had come to herself and was taking everything in, she had heard one of the assistants say, "I never saw so brave a woman;" and the other, "Oh, everybody knows where they get their courage!" and this had given her much pleasure. But she added, "After all, it was not courage: it was only a little love!"

CHAPTER XII.

THE operation succeeded. I shall say nothing here of the emotion with which we saw Adelaide again, the sensation which the sight of her frightful wound gave us, or of the tension continually renewed during the nine following days, when the possibility of hæmorrhage held her life by a thread. I shall only say that all that while, when she from time to time suffered dreadful pain, and when, if it was impossible to speak, it would have been easy to groan, not a complaint was heard, nor did a word escape feebly from her lips that was not a word of endearment or of thanksgiving. Once, after one of those painful dressings, she was seized with such spasms, that she joined her hands in silence almost convulsively, and with an expression of the keenest suffering; but a minute afterwards a smile broke upon her face. "It is over," she said; "I was sure that my dear Jesus would not let me suffer beyond my strength." The spasm, in truth, had ceased, and more than once she seemed to obtain by prayer a like immediate relief. It was a just reward, well due to her who asked so seldom, and almost always against the grain, to be spared.

At last Adelaide's recovery was complete, and after six weeks' stay she was able to leave Paris. Early in August she returned once more to her dear home at Bellavista, gladdened by the result of her journey, and making very light of the constant uneasiness and manifold pains which the rent and divided nerves of her face made her undergo, the paralysis of one side of it which ensued, and I must add, the reluctance she had to overcome in showing herself to the friends who had not seen her since the great change which had been made in her appearance. But she spoke of herself less than ever; and her mind, her goodness, and her grace remained not only the same as before, but it seemed as if her whole understanding and soul had enlarged. As her cheerfulness was unalterable, and she was soon able to take up again her usual occupations, and devote the same number of hours to her beloved niece, carrying on the same reading, and devoted to the same pursuits as formerly, her friends felt again thoroughly at ease about her. And it is nearly certain that she also felt satisfied about herself, or at least that she strove to be so, that she might be able to satisfy them. She even had the courage, just when so much past and actual suffering had enfeebled her strength, to take up a new pursuit. The paintings in the church had been done by herself, and now she undertook all the wood-carving with which it was to be decorated; and her work was so earnest, assiduous, and persistent, that she actually did accomplish a considerable quantity of carving, specially remarkable when the circumstances of its execution are considered.

The following winter Adelaide spent several months at Naples, where she took a more affectionate and motherly interest than ever in her nephews, on whose account she often drew her friends round her, which indeed cost her no effort; for to the very last she preserved the power of interesting herself so sincerely in every one who came near her, that the most trifling characters had often cause to think that their talk pleased her, so completely did her grand sweet disposition lend itself to others, and make itself all to all. Yet even during this time of supposed recovery, she never ceased to suffer the terrible consequences of the operation she had gone through; but to judge of the way in which she knew how to master bodily ailment, the letters, from which we shall quote later on, must be read.

When we recall that those bright, delightful, living pages—stirring and fresh with the keenest feelings that can be expressed—pages in which we find the very sparkle of youth renewed—fell from the pen of a person whose hearing, sight, and speech were affected, if not altogether, or so as to be apparent to others, yet enough to keep her in a state of weakness which was always discomfort, and often painful; when we recollect, moreover, that the very vigour which resisted disease added another discomfort; for, while she had her usual appetite, she could never eat without pain,—considering all this, I repeat again, we shall be forced to acknowledge that then, as before and as always, according to her desire and energetic expression, her soul, "that noble lady, was the mistress of her slave."

CHAPTER XIII.

"' From the Tower of Bellavista, July 16, 1867.*

"MY DEAREST LITTLE FRIEND,—They tell me that by the laws of metempsychosis Plato and you are identified. I have always loved Plato, because I have ever liked those that raise my life above the slough in which Adam has placed us; but if he lives again in you, ah, then 'the dear shell, within which that grand soul lives once more, is of double price, and I worship it.' *Questa cara larva, in cui vive ora l'anima di quel grande, radoppia il suo valore, e l'adoro.* When I say *worship*, it is only in jest; for indeed I worship only one God in Three Persons. Let me love you, then; but let it *only* be without measure. In answer to what you told us of the

* All these letters are to her niece, who had been some months married.

Marquis Fabio Pallavicini's wit, I send you the following saying, which is worthy of him, but is Azeglio's. He says that so long as we were under the rule of the *sovereign paternity*, he heartily wished to be an orphan; but now that the new government proclaims our brotherhood, he is miserable at not being an only son."

"Tower of Bellavista, Aug. 7, 1868.

"MOST PRECIOUS ONE,—I am painting three hours a day, and it amuses me. I caress you with the end of my brush; I softly kiss your brow and your cheeks; and then I think I am with you, and it does me good. Do you know this is the fourth picture I have drawn of you? One very so-so at two years old, another at sixteen, a third at twenty, and this which I am now busy about, just as you are four-and-twenty. I have promised your mother *to do one myself* when your hair is gray, and do not laugh at my presumption. Let my successors be furious, but I intend to live to be a hundred. This means that I am very well; so amuse yourself, and do not think about me.

"As for me, I amuse myself as an old woman should, and I say my prayers. The other morning I was saying a *Pater* for you, and while whispering over the Lord's Prayer to myself, I said, 'O my Father, Who art in Heaven, shall I ask Thee that Adelina may sanctify Thy Name? I trust she will sanctify it. That she may desire Thy kingdom to come? I believe that she does not fail to do so. That she may pray for Thy will to be done? Thine has been always hers, and will be so, *whatever may happen*. That she may forgive her enemies? She has done so since coming to the use of reason; there is no bitterness in her heart. Shall I pray that she be not led into temptation? Ah, yes, yes! O my Father, Who art in Heaven, let her never fall under temptation, and be kept from all evil. Amen, amen!'

"This is how I prayed for you—was it not

well done? Is not temptation the real danger of life? Is it not that downward incline upon which we may not set our foot? for the descent is rapid, and sin is at the bottom of it; sin, into which one so quickly falls, if we do not walk carefully.

"Last year I read something about the Etruscans, whose pedestal they are trying now—and perhaps justly—to pull down. I feel it difficult to strip myself of a single honour for the sake of the Pelasgi. But what is to be done? for we must submit to the necessities of history, though it overturns a great many of our notions and great names. History pulls down the proud, and exalts the lowly; saying to us very much what St. Remi said to the haughty Sicamber: 'Burn what you have worshipped, and worship all that you have burnt.'"

"Tower of Bellavista, Feb. 18, 1868.*

"Usurpation is the order of the day; so I

* Written in Italian.

take Clotilde's place, who was writing to you, and I am going to keep it. I have just finished a letter to Ernest at Florence, where he is busy about his future career, and no doubt will not answer my letter. No matter, for my *auntly* love—*amore zierno*—is like the motherly—unchangeable, and always the same. They both resemble an ever-living spring: when any one is thirsty, he comes to it to drink; but when he goes away, the spring flows on all the same."

"April 20, 1868.

"Come, my little friend, would you like to write a novel, and lay the scene in Calabria? This matter has never yet been treated *delicately*. It is always seasoned and *peppered* excessively, as if that were needed. The idea of Calabria is ever associated with brigands, according to the received notion of taking the exception for the rule. All I know is, that your letters from there *fill* me with a sweet, rather pensive feeling, that melancholy which poets call *malinconia, ninfa gentile!** The dance you describe, that magnificent country so deliciously southern,—all this, Mimi, Mimi of my heart, makes me long to be there with you! I do so love what is beautiful! and to me beauty has such wide bounds, that it causes me perpetual joy; for I find it easily, and relish it in all its degrees, from the graceful to the sublime. Everything that comes the least in the world *from above* brings with it a perfection and relative harmony without which there is no beauty, but with which everything is beautiful. Good-bye, farewell! I leave off to-day because I feel deeply, and words will not come —*e il mio dir corto.* This disturbance worries me, so I make an end."

"Tower of Bellavista, May 2, 1868.

"MY DEAR ADELINA,—This dear month of May is come, and I feel refreshed with all na-

---

* "Melancholy, thou gentle nymph!"

tural things; though when one thinks of it, what dreadful anniversaries occur in this month of Paradise! *El dos de Mayo*—the second of May—the massacre of the French at Madrid; on the 5th, Napoleon's death, which many people reckon as a misfortune; the 15th, another fatal day for Naples in 1848; and then the very idea of the 4th of May gives me the idea of chaos, of pandemonium, and of every uttermost confusion.* In spite of all this, long live the month of Mary! I liked it still better when I thought it would bring you back to us; but this will come later, and you will be *always* welcome. To-day we got your letter; and your letters are always so touching! I do believe that if you told us about Punch, Harlequin, Columbine, and every funniest thing in the world, it would bring little tears to our eyes. I do

* At Naples this is the day from which houses are let, and therefore that when all the removals and settlements take place.

not know why; perhaps it is the way in which love expresses itself. Ah, yes, it is the true, and tender, and strong love we feel for you, which spreads itself over everything that comes from you, wraps us round, thrills us through, stirs us up, and will go with us to Heaven. Clotilde would say to me, 'Do not run off the line so;' and she is right. It is enough for the handle of the blade to appear; the blade must remain hidden.

"But in speaking to you, Clotilde allows this both for me and herself."

"Tower of Bellavista, April 29, 1868.

"MY VERY DEAR ADELINA,—There are, as you know, the delights of spring; but spring has also its dark days, for this pretty season has a marked influence upon our spirits; sometimes toning them towards rose-colour, sometimes towards black; at least that happens to me. To-day I am joyous, while latterly I have been sad without any cause. Ah, how one good day blots out every shadow on the mind, and one enjoys in four-and-twenty hours what is enough to adorn a whole week! Everything then seems beautiful and easy. I went out walking this morning, and the shade was refreshing, and the sunshine enchanting. I went to see the Marchioness C——, whose little girl seemed to me a love, and she most kind and obliging. I settled two pieces of business—one for Ernest, the other to place out a little girl; both of which succeeded just as I wished. I am reading St. Paul's Epistles every morning in the tribune after Mass. To-day I read that to the Galatians, where he tells how he reproved St. Peter, who through weakness allowed circumcision for the Christians. With what courage St. Paul rebuked him for his cowardice! and how humbly did St. Peter listen and submit! *he* the first of the Apostles, upon whom Christ had founded His Church, while St. Paul seemed only one who had intruded on the twelve chosen, having not even learnt the Gospel from those who had the right to preach it! If these two great Saints had appeared to me yesterday, could they have impressed me more than they did to-day? *Non so.** On coming home, I went into the garden —that is, the so-called—and made a nosegay of mignonette, violets, and heliotrope. Had these flowers really the fragrance I feel they had, or was it only the influence of spring? I know not, dear Adelina of my heart; but I felt filled and enchanted with it.

"The last act of my spring delights to-day was this: I stayed one hour at the piano, taking the *Stabat Mater* of Pergolese. How delicious! I played the three first verses without singing, and mounted, mounted upwards to the first, second, third heaven! I was in the upper air when Clotilde came in. She took my place at the piano, and I sang *Quæ mærebat.* Ah, how beautiful it is! There is genius, imagination, know-

* I do not know.

ledge, feeling! I thank our good God for having allowed a simple mortal to mount so high, and to bring back to the world a ray of His beauty. The Promethean fable is a most true fiction. Man may steal the sacred fire — at least he can win it. He is not a creator, but he knows how to raise his works to a height which draws near to perfection; and then God condescends to breathe into them, and make them living. You see, dear friend, how I share with you the secrets of my being; you cannot say that with you I am buttoned up!"

"Tower of Bellavista, May 4, 1868.

"I am charmed that you are in Calabria, that you stay there, and that you are draining to the dregs what is delicious to the very last. But the month of May will soon be over; and then you will come back, and that will be an enchanting moment. While waiting for you, we are in the depths of Mons. Gobineau's book on Central Asia. It is shameful to find out how many things there are that one does not know the least. Did I know that there were celebrated schools of philosophy in Persia? That, while I write, there are excellent colleges at Ispahan, Khiva, and other places, where hundreds of scholars are collected to study philosophy; that professors abound; that his Excellency Hadji Moulla Hady de Sebzewar is an exceptional man of science, an accomplished master in metaphysics? No, I knew absolutely nothing of all this; and if I had been going to tell you my ideas upon Persia as it is, I should certainly have put it among the nations whose glories are of the past. I confess it. My knowledge ended with Avicenna—that is, with Avicenna's name, no more; and yet I considered myself rather a well-informed woman! But I come down every day in my own eyes; and the more I learn, the more ignorant I feel. Ah, Pascal was right when he said, that the highest degree of human knowledge was to know that one knows nothing."

"Tower of Bellavista, May 10, 1867.

"I perfectly understand your pleasant feeling in chatting with your two young friends. That peaceful country life and the long hours of talk expand the heart; and certain recesses for ever closed, except then, are mutually opened. And it is good to penetrate them, for they contain the key to the riddle of character; and it is always interesting to make an entrance there. We like to know the unknown. Curiosity—the motive-power of many good things, when taken on its good side—is satisfied, as it would be by the discovery of an unknown land, and we like to cut a road through it. So we love to get into the mysterious corners of another's heart, where one always finds a crowd of matters of which one has not dreamed. In these secret hiding-places we find out the distinguishing marks between two people, who in the eye of the world seem alike; for it would be impossible to class the world into categories or individualities. I own that the charm of thus diving into a heart laid open to me has been one of the greatest pleasures of my life; so much so, that in my young days, finding it dangerous, I denied myself this pleasure.

"Shall I tell you what has latterly given me something of a kindred pleasure? It is the discovery of Indian literature. We have become acquainted with the turns of thought, the belief, and the various feelings of this great people; not through any trick or cunning, but because their books have suddenly been opened to us. What treasures, what things we neither knew of nor imagined! We knew the Indian race had been highly civilised, but what did our knowledge consist in? That they were philosophers and poets. But what they really thought, said, and did, this is what we thought nothing about, but which we now know to the smallest detail. Each beautiful mind that opens to us is an India which we have discovered. But, alas, the comparison fails, for there are few souls in whom we find such greatness! My dear Adelina, how difficult it is to stop when once I begin to chat with you! The regions of thought are your kingdom, and I find myself with you there in such good company! But I must bring you back to this world again. You want to know about my health. What shall I say? There is nothing to be told about a stationary condition. On the whole, I am not ill; but in particular, I am like a clock-pendulum, which goes backwards and forwards, and remains always in the same place."

"Tower of Bellavista, May 12, 1868.

" I have always remarked, that if a correspondence lasts and does not die of inanition, it must either be sustained by deep affection, or by common interests, or by some common literary taste. Adelina, darling, we are united by these three bonds, and thus our correspondence does not dry up; and I wish that my letters may be received with a quarter of the interest that yours give to me. Your last, filled with Alban details, interested us amazingly. Those Alban things always excited my curiosity, and I so wished to know how far they have retained their characteristics, shut in as they were by Calabrian territory. What an interesting country, classical in all times and in every respect! At this moment, however, I am thoroughly wrapt up in the history of the Bâbys in Persia. That part of Mons. Gobineau's work is infinitely interesting. It seems to me that I read formerly in some paper an account of the phases of that great religious revolution, but without paying the smallest attention to it, and most likely without understanding it; for one understands the least about things that are happening in our own day.

"You are not coming yet, after all? Perhaps you will come for St. Clotilde? Anyhow, everything that *is*, is right to be so. I know that you want to see us; I know that you long to see your brother again, and to become acquainted with your sister-in-law; but I know too that you like to do what it is your duty to do; and God will bless you."

"Tower of Bellavista, May 15, 1868.

"MY VERY DEAR ADELINA,—I will not talk about your coming home. I know you wish it, and you know how much we wish for it. But it is useless to be occupied about it; for certainly it will be when it can be, and our wishes will not hasten the time. I know that Cillo* will do all he can to make you happy; so I shall be silent upon the matter, though it is what we are chiefly thinking about. In the second place, there is our reading. Decidedly, if one were so wretched as not to be

* The Count de Melissa.

a Christian, one would be a Bâbys. It is a religion harmonising with our notions, though in some things very droll. For instance, Bâb, who was the Mahomet of the sect, was a special protector of women and children. In his care for women in general, he commends all those who were betrothed to the faithful, and desires that ornaments, and everything that can add to their gladness and beauty, should be lavished upon them, saying: 'Decorate your adornment, and honour your glory.' Then he strongly reprobates those who ill-treat children: 'If thou desirest to be of the number of the faithful, strike [children] very gently, nor smite thy scholar before he is over five years old. If thou then wilt strike him, give him no more than five blows, and those not upon the flesh, unless there be a hand or some covering between the rod and his flesh.' Is not this charming? How full these particulars are of good feeling!"

"Tower of Bellavista, May 18, 1868.

"Goodness! the rule-and-line exactness of the B——s used in past times to irritate my nerves, and sudden decisions took a high place in my esteem. The benefits of things settled without foregone arrangements seemed to me infinitely preferable. 'But wise men have changed their ideas with the times.'* I did not then know the *hideous* inconvenience of the contrary fault; and now I ban it, and desire that it should be put beyond the pale of the law. Let the fiend of *indecision* be anathematised; and while all mercy is shown to the sinners, let the sin be held up to detestation!

"Now I know that you are going to stay in Calabria, I shall actively carry on our correspondence; for I should not like my letters to fail you. Poor Don Jerome has lost his brother. It is very sad; for a brother's love is not easily replaced. Still I think he will be

---

* "*Ma cangiano i saggi, secondo i tempi, i lor pensieri.*"

like a great many others in this very impressionable country, and that time will do its work on him as for them. The violent grief of a day, and then a fresh life, when the wind blows and carries away the past. This is certainly not the wind of Dante's Lucifer, which froze the tears in the eyes of the lost, and thus for ever stamped their grief upon them. This transitory impression of the bitterest grief in our Southern countries has always served me with food for the deepest thought. The whole charge of trouble seems to explode at once. People are rent with grief; they are overwhelmed, annihilated, drowned by it; but if you do not break down under the first hour's trials, they are got over, and very soon ended. This is, no doubt, providential; but it is not pleasant to see. It is the failure of all human things, the saddest and least poetic side on which to look at it.

"Nevertheless, I do like sometimes to know

that the most violent sorrows are not eternal. If not for this, what would become of that wretched Strato, at the coffee-shop, and his wife, whose child has come to a dreadful end? A delicious pet of six years old, the glory of the infant-school. One of his schoolfellows, not knowing what he was doing, poked a carooba-seed into his ear about a month ago. They were never able to get it out, and he died in dreadful pain. Listen, Mimi darling; if ever you have any children, I shall make them little caps to tie under their chins, that their dear little ears may be out of all harm!"

"Tower of Bellavista, May 21, 1868.

"It is a very sad and touching thing to see the poor monks, who have been driven out of their convents, taking up again some rough trade, by which they may gain a living. This morning I felt so much at seeing poor Brother Alphonsus, the Trinitarian, carpentering. Another is weaving, and so on. No doubt labour is a grand thing, and any one who lends himself to it is to be honoured. But the life of an artisan is painful; and when I think of that idea—'*Shall I get bread to-day? to-morrow?*'—being inflicted upon so many poor religious, who lived so entirely sheltered from all care for the morrow, it makes my heart ache. O, how that persistent thought of to-morrow must wear them out! What a wicked and foolish act it was to suppress them! Listen, Adelina: there is but one thing I hate more than disorder, and that is destruction."

CHAPTER XIV.

THERE is certainly nothing to be found in these letters which could lead any one to guess that a fatal change had come about in Adelaide's health; and yet some months before the date of the last, pain and other too well-known symptoms had come to warn her that the enemy was not overcome, and then to convince her that it had conquered. In short, the pitiless disease was reasserting its fatal course; and Adelaide knew it, and was resigned to the knowledge. If we admire her courage three years before, when the first indication of evil had shown itself, we must now wonder at it much more, when the trial had reappeared, aggravated by the many attempts at cure, by so much suffering, and by so many vain hopes. Now there was no longer any room for doubt. She had accepted suffering with patience; had gone through the painful cure with energy; had welcomed hope with joy, and had beheld ner life renewed with thanksgiving. But now death clearly showed itself to be the ever-blessed will of God; and as she had accepted the suffering and the cure, the hopes and their failure, so she accepted death also, without weakness, without hesitation, and without complaint.

From this moment that already grand soul began to develop more and more, and each successive day to make known from what Divine source she drew her courage, what support hindered her from failing, and, above all, what was that strength which had caused her, with such firm faith, to believe that her weakness could endure *all things.* At the beginning of this relapse, as at the outset of her illness, she changed nothing of her outward life; nothing betrayed anxiety or trouble. The only resolution she took was not to undergo another operation; but she consented to follow a course of treatment, which she undertook as if she had hopes of its success, and so spoke of it as to induce others to hope also.

That year—1867—Christmas-eve was celebrated at Bellavista with great solemnity. The tribune in which Adelaide heard Mass every day led out of a gallery to her room; she could thus assist at all the ceremonies, which gave her inexpressible joy. She said to me: "I thought I should not have strength for it; and I so reckoned on it; for I do think it will be my last Christmas on earth." But scarcely had this inner thought escaped her when she quickly added: "I beg of you not to say a word to Pauline," her eldest sister.

Towards the spring the disease somewhat abated; and when I went away she said: "If you come back before the autumn, you will find me here still." But when she saw what pain these words gave me, she smiled and said: "You will see that I shall not suffer too much; the disease will spread too rapidly, perhaps even suddenly. If not, God will help me. His will be done!"

This was the end of everything to her. But to enter into the strength of the words from her lips, and at the time they were uttered, we must call to mind the terms in which she spoke to Adelina of her submission to God's will, and remember that now the cruel disease of which she was dying threatened to become a wound, and to cover her whole face. Certainly many of the best, and bravest, and most resigned to death might have trembled in such a case at the thoughts of all that might come to aggravate death; but Adelaide did not blench; she went straight forward along the path of acceptance without looking back; and God allowed the peace of perfect detachment to become more and more shining in her bright soul.

The only special request she made at this time of her sisters, her friends, and all whom she knew, was, never to ask that she might be cured.

This thorough submission would appear more surprising if I could have better described her state of activity, and moral and intellectual enjoyment, when this terrible disease seized her in keen health. Her years had neither injured her, nor robbed her of her bloom, nor chilled in the very least her heart; and she would have rejoiced to live with a thankfulness equal to the submission with which she accepted death. But that we may acknowledge in all things the goodness of God, it must be added that if He laid upon her one hard trial, He spared her those which she would have found a thousand times more terrible. She was conscious of bodily disease in its severest shape, but she never knew the grief of outliving those she loved; and if she had been called upon to choose her cross, we feel sure she would have chosen that which she carried rather than the other.

While death drew near with slow but relentless steps, Adelaide calmly pursued her ordinary course of life. As long as she could raise her arm without suffering too much, she painted and carved. When this labour was beyond her strength, she read and studied; and when she grew too weak to read herself, she listened to others reading, and seemed to take the same interest as ever in these pursuits. In that submission to God's will, which is the most perfect preparation for death as well as the perfection of life, if she had been told that she should die before the end of the day, she would certainly have said, like St. Aloysius Gonzaga, that she could do no other than she was doing.

Nothing apparently changed in her state of health for some months; but at the end of the year her sadly stationary condition suddenly took a new and worse aspect; but although the danger became more imminent, the disease was less painful, having changed its nature; and while the sufferer's courage never gave way, even when long agonies seemed in store for her, it became less trying to her friends to see the malady—probably from the effect of treatment—changed into rapid consumption.

Remembering, then, that her people might rather wish her to die among them, she resolved to leave that beautiful bay, upon which she had fondly hoped her eyes might rest to the last, and her beloved home, where, a few months before, she had blessed God for allowing her to end her days, and to take a small lodging in Naples, where she might breathe her last. It may be, too, that she wished to avoid the too sad recollections for the survivors, which would cling to Bellavista; but, be that as it may, she carried out this sacrifice with her usual courage, concealing, even from the faithful companion of her life, what it cost her. But when the time came for their departure, thinking that she was alone in the drawing-room—so crowded with memorials of friendship, study, and devotion, and where so many happy hours had been spent—she was seen to go up to the walls and kiss them.

After this farewell, she and her sister took their way to Naples, looking back once only at the sea, the mountains, Vesuvius, and all that enchanting scene which had been the magnificent framework of her simple and noble life. On the 24th December 1868, Adelaide came to Naples to finish her generous and courageous, and I might almost say her *joyful* sacrifice; for in the worst of the cruellest agonies she sometimes cried out: "O, what joys, what joys are these! not human, but Divine!"* "Do you

* "*O, che delizie, che delizie son queste! non umane, ma Divine!*"

know," she said again, one of the last days of her life, "do you know the real inscription to carve upon a tomb? It is *Janua Cœli*,"—Gate of Heaven.

Even then she scarcely ever spoke of her approaching end, that she might spare others; but having wished to see a young English girl, a servant to one of her friends, who had nursed her well and faithfully three years before at Paris, and who was going away, she said to her, "Eliza, I wanted to see you again, to thank you once more, and to say good-bye to you. In less than a month's time I shall be no longer here; *but do not say this to any one.*" Seeing the girl's eyes fill with tears, Adelaide said, "Ah, do not be grieved; I am so glad! It will be so beautiful up there! so beautiful; and we shall be so happy!" Then she changed the subject, and obliged the girl to answer her, listening to her with a smile; and after hearing one of her stories, said, "Ah, I should laugh heartily if it were not for this;" pointing patiently to her poor scarred and ever-aching cheek.

She kept up in the same way until the day on which she asked for the Last Sacraments. After that time, without losing her calm, she put away her constraint, and spoke of her death openly and simply to us all.

She received Extreme Unction and the Viaticum, and a great number of the poor of Posilippo and Bellavista having come in tears to see her and bid her farewell, the venerable priest who attended her begged her to receive them. They came in, and to each one she spoke a kind word and gave some last advice. "Remember," she said to a prisoner whose discharge she had obtained, " remember to conduct yourself always well." They begged her to give them her blessing; "she shrugged up her shoulders, smiling, with a gesture of humility, as if they were not in earnest; but then she obeyed their wish, and lifting up her hand, still most beautiful in spite of the emaciation of sickness, she made the sign of the Cross over them all." These words I quote from her beloved niece, who above all others had been moulded by the impress of the soul now leaving this world.

The struggle with death was long-continued, and Adelaide seemed to beseech the forgiveness of all who suffered at seeing her suffer, and could not understand why her God so delayed His coming. "I am grieving you all," she said, "and here am I, happy among you!" She was pained when with her eldest sister, seeing her suffer so much; while to Clotilde, her inseparable companion, she spoke sweet words, still avoiding too much emotion. Once with great earnestness she said to her niece and nephew, who were always with her, "I commend my Lolé to you"—her pet name for Clotilde—"do not let her be too much alone." And when they bade her be quite happy on that score, she replied, "O, I am happy; for you know very well that I have never spoken about this till now." To Adelina and Ernest she repeated, "I recommend the straight course to you both, everywhere and always." By this she always meant, to them, the practice of religion. Even in these solemn moments she preserved that graceful charm which had always characterised her. Her maid once came in, saying that she was dying of cold; when Adelaide smiled, and observed, "One comes in saying she is dying of cold, and another that she is dying of fatigue; I really think I am the only one among you who is alive."

Her sufferings, nevertheless — the terrible effect of the disease, which, while checked outwardly, was undermining her vital powers — were sometimes excessive; but when, in spite of her efforts, she could not help crying out, she said, "My good God, it is only my nerves that scream! I am glad to suffer, and to suffer for Thee." Another time, when in an agony of sharp pain, she exclaimed, "O my God! I do not ask for any respite, but I do beg of Thee to give me courage."

The day but one before her death, the sharp suffering ceased, and she looked upon this relief as the forerunner of her end. "The word agony," she said, "seems terrible at a distance; but if I am in my agony, it is very sweet."

Crowds of friends came one after another, anxious to show their love, and to obtain from her at least a single word of farewell. She spoke to them all in turn, and to each with some distinguishing mark of affection. On her lips the sweet diminutives of the South sounded sweeter than ever; and very many times were the names of Nina, Dora, Maria, Giuditalla, *Carmensita dulce*,[*] with such-like others, pro-

---

[*] Princess Torella, the young Duchess di Balzo, the Mar-

nounced by her during her last days on earth. No one who knew her could doubt that every one of these friends had each some word, some thought, some special prayer, or that she bore with her the remembrance of each to love them in Heaven as she had loved them on earth; for she was thoroughly convinced that death cuts off nothing, but merely changes the holy affections of earth by giving them full power as well as unending life.

So, at last, the hour of Adelaide's blessed rest had come; the hour which she had distinctly named a whole day before; the hour of passage from this perishable life to that glorious and immortal state for which she had lived.

It was on the 9th of January, at half-past three o'clock, while surrounded by every one dear to her on earth; her two sisters, those

chioness Bugnano, the Marchioness di Montesilvano, the Duchess di Bivona, whose name was Carmen, and to whom she always spoke in Spanish, "My sweet little Carmen."

whom she called her children, one kneeling beside her, holding her hand, and the other supporting her drooping head. Thus she yielded her soul, without pain, after once more uttering the words so often heard during her illness: *In Te, Domine, speravi; non confundar in æternum.* "In Thee, O Lord, I have hoped; I shall not be confounded for ever."

* * * * *

O thou dear and noble soul! gentle and strong, now joined to so many other among the blessed, pray, oh pray with them for all those whom thou didst so love on earth!

The Southern custom—so unlike the usages of the North—banishes the nearest relations immediately from the bedside of their dead, and forbids them even to follow them to the grave; for the very vehemence of their grief renders them habitually incapable of acting like those who are accustomed to master and overcome their feelings. This custom, however, gives its special day of pious devotedness to friendship, as what is forbidden to the relations is imposed as a kind of obligation upon the friends; and some are chosen from among them to perform those painful duties which are usually left in others' hands. All Adelaide's friends were inclined to claim this mournful privilege; and there were several who, in the end, agreed to share the sad offices which follow death. The post of remaining beside the remains fell upon two friends, whose long intimacy and devoted affection gave it them almost as a right. These friends of her childhood and youth—Euphemia and Elizabeth Fonton—were two sisters, who, having lost a third sister, whom they deeply loved, had given up the world, to carry on, in almost nun-like retirement, those good works which belong to the heroism of charity. In this way their love and sorrow had long induced them to lead that kind of life together in seclusion which

Adelaide and Clotilde led in society; and they had always maintained their mutual intimacy. Now therefore they presented themselves with loving reverence to fulfil the last great duty of friendship; but they were not alone, for a third friend, much younger than these two— the Duchess Ravaschieri Fieschi—came to join them. She had been struck down, in the bloom of life, by one of those blows which, if they do not blight by hopelessness or a heartless dissipation, stamp the soul with a special seal, and open to it higher and purer regions, where peace, if not happiness, may be regained. This young mother had lost her only child— an angelic creature, whom others besides herself can never forget—and had been linked to Adelaide by that sympathy of noble souls which draws them together, and forms closer ties than those of blood. She also shared the sad satisfaction of fulfilling those last duties which were all that remained to them now.

Their hands prepared the body of Adelaide for burial, and laid it upon a bed covered with flowers and shaded by no funeral draperies; for she had expressly desired that the customs of Naples should not be observed in her instance. They, therefore, left her room in its usual way, and everything about the dear remains wore its ordinary, simple, peaceful, and bright look, like the soul of which they were the shell, whose impress had not been the least changed by death.

Then, after her own beloved people had kissed her for the last time, the neighbours, the peasants whom she had loved, and the needy whom she had helped, came to pray beside her. Then, too, were heard sobs and cries mingled with prayers, for grief with the Neapolitans is as noisy and expansive as their joy. Among the exclamations which echoed on all sides, a poor woman of Posilippo was heard to exclaim, "*Go then, go to thy home, thou beautiful bit of Paradise!*" and we should not like to leave out this lowly but vivid expression of belief in her immediate happiness. Adelaide's three friends then placed her in the coffin, and these same three followed her to her last resting-place.

In another day this resting-place would have been the magnificent chapel where her forefathers lie, and the great doors of the Cathedral of Naples, above which stands the lion of their shield, would have opened as in former times, and for them alone, to let them pass to their rest.* Now her burial-place is a lowlier one; but the sweet recollections which hover about it yield more honour than that splendid fane to the name she bore, to the land that she loved, to the holy faith which she practised, and to the God Whom she so loved, and Who crowned her with reward.

* Note B.

NOTES.

A.

Don Bernardo, Count de Galvez, Viceroy of Mexico, Adelaide Minutolo's maternal grandfather, had earned an honourable name during the war, in 1781, between England with France and Spain. The town of Pensacola, defended by two forts which bar the entrance to the gulf of the same name, was about to be invested. The Count de Galvez, seeing that the commanders of both the French and Spanish fleets hesitated to enter the gulf, passed into the strait himself with his single corvette, gained the town—which is at the end of the gulf—under a storm of shot, and as the two fleets followed his lead, Pensacola surrendered.

In commemoration of this action the King of Spain empowered Don Bernardo to add a corvette to his arms, with the motto, "*Yo solo*, I alone;" to which the French King added the royal lily, or fleur-de-lys of France. He was afterwards made Viceroy of Mexico *for life*. His frank, noble, and generous character made him universally beloved; and when carried off by a premature death, he was universally regretted by both his province and all his friends.

Don Bernardo laid the foundations of the famous castle of Tchapultepec, raised on one of the heights which overlook the city of Mexico. The next Viceroy, who was unpopular, gave out that the Count de Galvez had his own ambitious designs in building this castle; but the manner in which his widow was received by the King and Spanish court on her return to Europe entirely destroyed this slander. The castle or fort of Tchapultepec was completed by the late unfortunate Emperor Maximilian.

B.

Stephen II. (Capece), the Doge and Bishop of Naples, founded this chapel in the cathedral as far back as the eighth century, dedicating it to the Apostle St. Peter. The chapel was enriched by Cardinal Henry Capece Minutolo in the fourteenth century, and adorned with portraits of all the knights and warriors of the family, with their scutcheons.

This Cardinal Henry almost entirely rebuilt the Cathedral of Naples. The great entrance, and the statue of the Cardinal kneeling, which is over it, were carved by Barocci di Piperno. The Cardinal's tomb is at the end of the chapel; on the right is that of Orso Capece Minutolo, Archbishop of Salerno; on the left that of Philip Capece Minutolo, Archbishop of Naples, who died in 1301. This Archbishop's ring was stolen after his death, which forms the chief incident in Boccaccio's tale of Andreuccio di Perugia. After 420 years of burial, Philip Minutolo's tomb was opened, and his body was found flexible and entire; it was then placed in another tomb.

In 1345, when the unfortunate King Andrew, the husband of Queen Joan I. of Naples, was assassinated at Avversa, Ursillo Capece Minutolo, of the same family, guarded his remains, and placed them in the next chapel to his own, putting up also a monument to his memory which is now in the cathedral. Cardinal Henry died in 1412; and from that time the Minutolo family actually held this special right over the great entrance to the

L

Cathedral, that it was never opened unless one of their race passed in to be buried in their own mortuary chapel.

The family is now divided into three branches: the Princes of Ruoti, the oldest of all; the Princes of Canosa, to whom Adelaide belonged; and the Dukes of San Valentino.

The Capece family were constant adherents of the House of Suabia; and in 1286, a little while before the defeat and death of Manfred, Marino and Carado Capece entertained him in their castle of Atrapaldi, near Avellino, with almost royal hospitality. Marino was afterwards the constant companion of Conradin, shared his sufferings to the last, and died with him on the scaffold, in 1288.

After this event, the name of Capece became perilous on account of the hatred of the conquering party, and the family adopted or restored that of *Minutolo,* which they have ever since borne.

It is not my place, nor would it in any way become me, to enlarge upon the feelings which their great loss excites in Adelaide's family. I cannot, however, resist inserting the following page of

Goethe, translated by the niece to whom nearly all the foregoing letters were written; for this quotation seems to complete the letters. We recognise how entirely she who chose out this passage for translation appreciated the affection lavished upon her, and feel therefore what exquisite enjoyment this must have caused Adelaide in return.

There is nothing rarer, indeed, than perfect sympathy between two people, one of whom is on the threshold of life, and the other advanced in years; but when we do meet with this fact, when two separate ages so mingle in one, combining all the choicest elements of life, nothing can be sweeter than the happiness produced.

May this thought soften in some degree the very sadness which it stirs up!

"Ah, why has the friend of my youth left me? Why have I been made to know what she was? I ought to say to myself, 'Thou art a fool, seeking here what is no longer to be found!' But I have at least possessed this friend; I have known this heart; I have discerned this grand soul, in whose presence I felt myself greater ● myself, because with her I grew to the utmost height of which I was capable, and none of the powers of my soul lay dormant. When with her, I felt a wonderful power unfold within me, which seemed able to contain the whole natural world. Our conversation was an interchange of the deepest emotions of the heart, and the clearest thoughts of the mind; for in her everything, even her lightest sally of wit, was full of genius. And now, alas, the very years which she possessed over and above me have led her before me to the grave! I shall never forget her. Never can I forget the strength of her soul, and her Heavenly indulgence for me."

PAULINE CRAVEN.

Cava dei Tirreni, June 1869.

THE END.

Rob___ nd Sons, Printers, Old St. Pancras Road.

www.ingramcontent.com/pod-product-compliance
Lightning Source LLC
Chambersburg PA
CBHW030337170426
43202CB00010B/1150